technology WHY?

WHY DO MOBILE PHONES VIBRATE?

Om KIDZ
An imprint of Om Books International

WHY?

CONTENTS

Find out!

How is clean water supplied to water slides?

1 Why are trampolines bouncy?

It's the springs that make it bouncy. A trampoline has a strong fabric fitted into a metal frame with a number of steel springs on the side or under it. When you jump on the trampoline, the springs are pushed downward. They then pull back against your weight. As they return to their normal position, the fabric is pulled back into its original location and the taut fabric pushes you into the air!

Pocket fact

The first trampoline was built by George Nissen in his garage in 1936. He came up with the idea when he observed trapeze artists performing tricks while they bounced off of the safety net.

2 Why does a water slide have curved edges?

To keep you moving forward! Water slides have curved edges so that they propel you forward and gravity keeps your movement going. If the slides did not have these curves, you would be launched into the air at the first turn. When you reach a turn while on the ride, you feel a strong force acting on your body. This force increases your speed when you move forward after crossing the turn. So, you smoothly move in a different direction.

Find out!

Where is the Peppermint Water Tower?

3 Why don't skyscrapers fall?

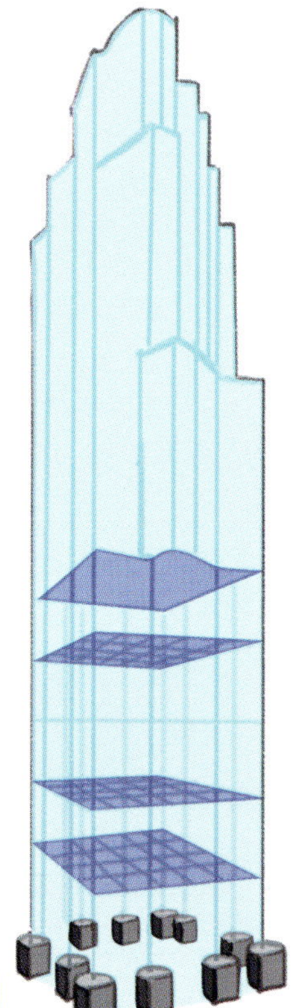

A lot of factors work together to keep them standing! The base of a skyscraper is supported by an underground substructure. A skyscraper's weight is supported by a group of strong vertical steel columns. These steel columns are built like three-dimensional grids, transferring the weight of the building directly to the vertical columns. Each floor is supported by horizontal steel gliders placed between the vertical columns. The walls on the outside are made of glass and concrete that add strength and make the skyscrapers look beautiful as well!

Pocket fact

Burj Khalifa, in Dubai, UAE, was declared the world's tallest building in 2010. It is 2,716 feet (828 metres) and has 160 storeys. It has the world's fastest elevator, and is estimated to use about 250,000 gallons of water everyday!

4 Why don't water towers freeze solid in very cold places?

They have heating systems! Water towers in very cold places have heating systems within the tank design. Water tanks have a central pipe called riser that runs up from the ground level up in to the bottom of the tank. Water is pumped into the base of the riser and allowed to rise into the tank. These risers are wrapped with heat tape, covered with insulation and capped by an aluminum jacket so that water doesn't freeze in the tank!

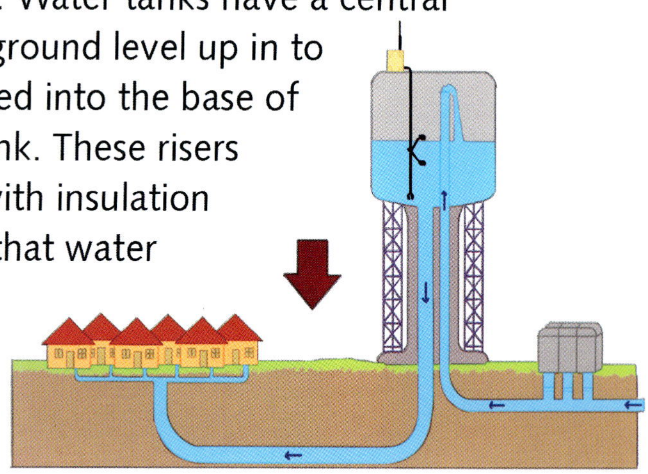

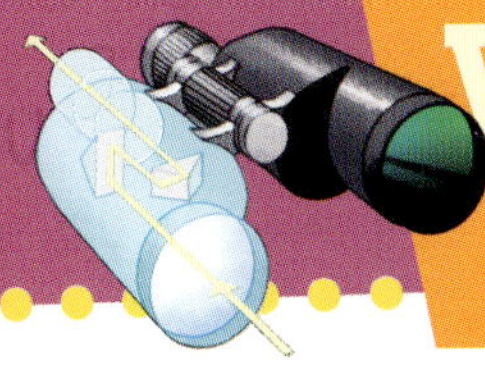

Find out!

Why do bottles have necks?

5 Why do some soft drink bottles have bumps at the bottom?

To increase the strength of the bottles! When a liquid is cooled, its volume changes. This change in volume can make the bottle buckle. Bending any material increases its strength and rigidity. Since soft drinks are mostly served chilled, their bottles are made with bumps or corrugations at the bottom to increase their strength. The corner or the tip of the bump can slightly expand/contract without breaking when there is a change in volume of the soft drink.

6 Why do dams have spillways?

To provide safe release of the water before it overflows! Spillways are structures constructed on dams so that water can be safely released from the dam to a downstream. A dam built on a river has a reservoir to store water. When the reservoir is full, the water level goes up. This may result in over-topping of the dam. To avoid this, water must be passed to the downstream. This is done by providing a spillway which draws water from the top of the reservoir and prevents the dam from over-topping.

Pocket fact

Hoover Dam was built on river Colorado in 1935. It was the most expensive dam built at that time in the history of the United States. Its construction cost around $49 million.

Find out!

Why do the hands of a clock move from right to left?

7 Why do some wrist bands glow in the dark?

They contain phosphor! Phosphor is a chemical that radiates visible light when it is energised after being exposed to light. While making these bands, the phosphor is mixed with a radioactive element (usually tritium or promethium) that energises the phosphor continuously. This makes these bands glow in the dark!

8 Why do some watches make a 'ticking' sound?

Pocket fact

A glow stick or glow band does not require battery or electricity to generate light so they don't produce heat. They don't burn your hand so you can carry them safely!

A spring, balance wheel, gears, escapement and other small wheels work together to make the 'tick' sound! Not all watches, just the mechanical ones make the 'tick' sound. A mechanical watch uses a spring called a mainspring which must be wound periodically. The gears of the watch power the balance wheel which oscillates back and forth at a fixed rate. The escapement makes the small wheels move forward with each swing of the balance wheel. This moves the watch's hands forward at a fixed rate producing the tick sound you hear!

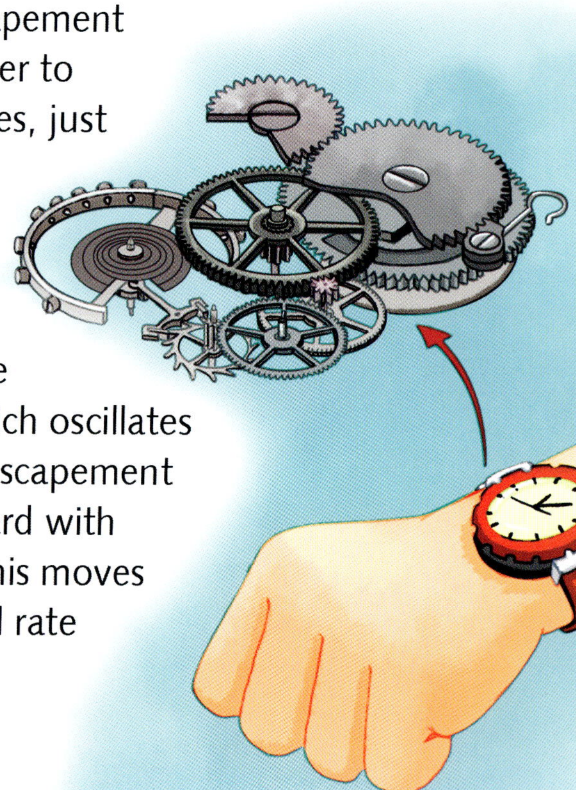

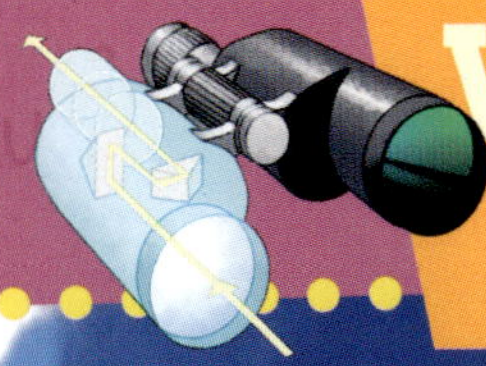

Find out!

From where has the word camera been derived?

9 Why does a camera have flash?

To brighten a dark scene! A flash is used in photography to produce a flash of artificial light that helps brighten a scene. Flashes are also used to capture quickly moving objects or to change the quality of light while taking a photograph.

Pocket fact

The first digital camera was designed in December 1975 by an engineer, Steve Sasson. It weighed eight pounds and produced black and white pictures at just 0.01 megapixels!

10 Why do we get red eyes in some photographs?

Because of retina! Your eyes have a layer called retina (at the back of the eyeball) that is rich in blood vessels. Red eyes may appear in photographs when you are either too close to a camera lens or the flash occurs too quickly for the pupil of your eyes to close. Light from the camera's flash goes through to the retina and strikes the red blood vessels. These blood vessels reflect the red colour and your eyes appear red in the photograph.

Find out!

What are the two major designs of binoculars?

11 Why do we use binoculars?

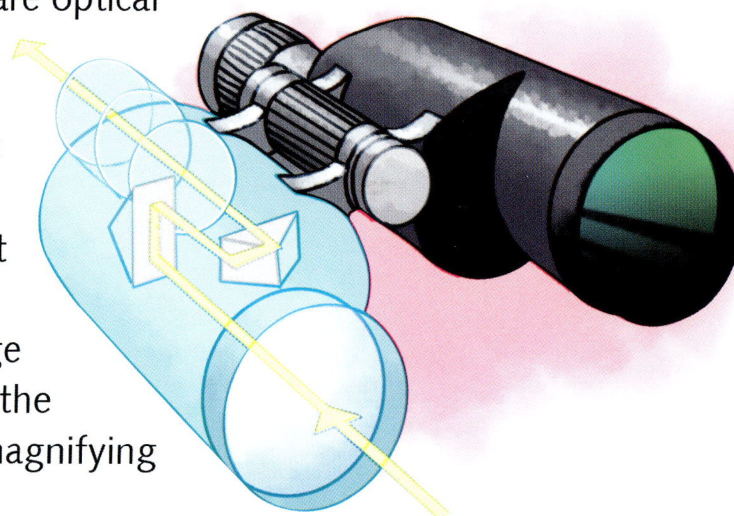

To see faraway objects! Binoculars are optical instruments with eyepiece lens, front lens and prisms. Light from a distant object reaches the front lens and makes a focused image at a short distance behind the lens. Light now passes through the prisms that refract the light and rotate the image formed. The eyepiece lens picks up the image and magnifies it, just like a magnifying glass magnifies an image on paper.

Pocket fact

The first barcode symbology was created in 1952 by Bernard Silver and Norman Joseph Woodland. This barcode symbology looked just like a bullseye!

12 Why are barcodes black and white?

So that they can be read accurately at high speeds! A barcode on any item is a unique number that is read by an electronic scanning device. It has a pattern of black and white stripes because white areas of the barcode reflect the most light and black areas reflect the least. When a scanner scans the code, light reflects back off the barcode into a photoelectric cell inside the barcode reading machine. This creates a pattern of 0 (for white) and 1 (for black) in the computer thus identifying the code easily and quickly!

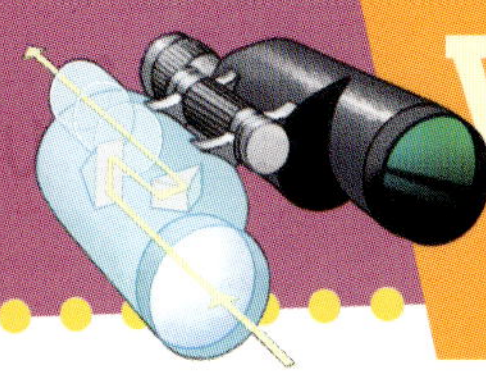

Find out!

When was the first smart phone developed?

13 Why do mobile phones vibrate?

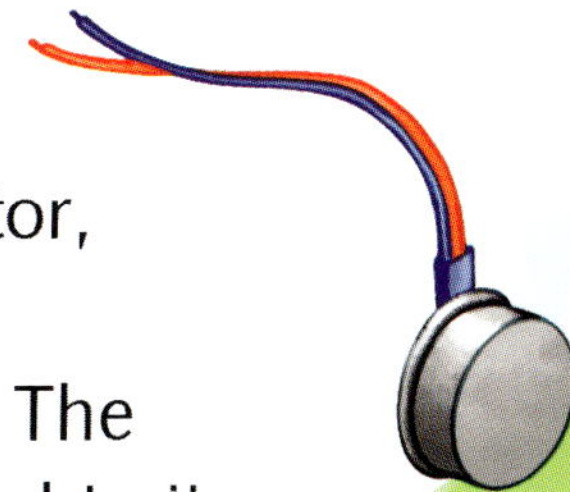

An unbalanced disc makes it vibrate! Mobile phones have a small direct current (DC) motor, which converts electricity into mechanical energy and a gear. The motor drives the gear connected to it. This gear has a small weight which is not placed at its centre. This makes the gear behave like an unbalanced disc. When you receive any call or alert, the disc rotates at high speed creating heavy vibrations. The vibration is transmitted to the body of the phone and thus it vibrates!

Pocket fact

The first photo using a mobile was shared by a French inventor Philippe Kahn in 1997. He sent pictures of his daughter Sophie from the hospital. He is credited to have developed the world's first camera phone.

14 Why do some mobile phones need a SIM card?

Because it holds a lot of critical information! A SIM card is a small card which contains a chip that must be inserted into GSM phones to make them work. The most important data that a SIM card has, is the information about the mobile service provider and the authentication key that validates it. When you insert a SIM card in a mobile, the network generates a number. If the network's number matches the SIM card's number, then the SIM card starts working!

Find out!

Are there any cars that don't have gears?

15 Why do race cars have bald tyres?

To reduce friction! A car has tyres that have a pattern of deep grooves called tyre treads. These make a car slower because of increased friction between the tyres and the road. But race cars don't have these treads, that's why their tyres are called bald. This makes the tyres smooth to allow the race cars to have more speed. Interestingly, these tyres need to be changed three to four times during a race as the baldness of the tyres wear them off easily.

Pocket fact

During a race, tyres lose weight. Each tyre loses about 0.5 kg weight due to wear and tear.

16 Why do cars have gears?

To control the power of engine transmitted to the wheels! The power generated by a car engine is very high, and you need to use this power in different ways while driving. For example, if you are driving in traffic, you cannot drive at high speed and need to slow down. Gears help you use this power in different ways and control the speed of the car. If a car does not have gears, it will always move at the constant speed that is very high!

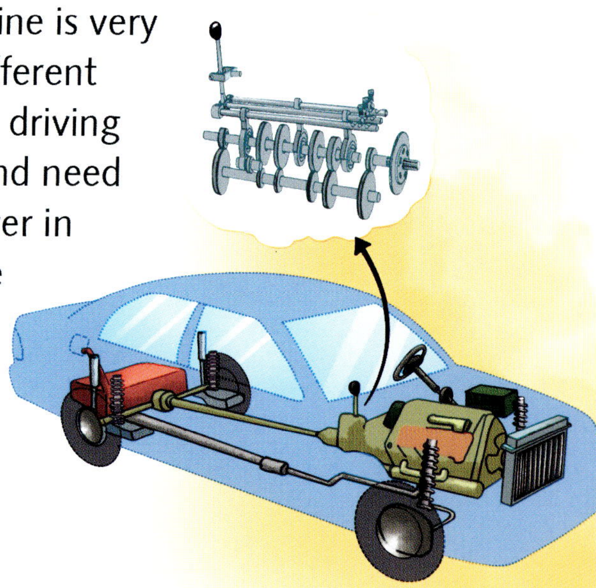

Find out!

Which is the world's fastest aeroplane?

17 Why do planes have rounded or curved windows?

To save them from cracking! An aircraft fuselage, the main body section that holds crew and passengers or cargo, experiences a lot of force when it rises from land to higher altitude. It has to hold in a lot of pressure, which makes it flex slightly. If an aircraft had square windows, a lot of pressure would be focused on the corners of the windows that would make them crack, which may lead to a crash. Windows with curved or rounded edges lessen the pressure, thus saving them from being cracked.

Pocket fact

The first airplane was invented and flown by the Wright brothers in 1903. It was named the Wright Flyer, and flew about 120 feet high.

18 Why do aeroplanes use special fuel?

For many reasons! Aircrafts use kerosene and paraffin oil-based fuel JET A-1 or a kerosene-naphthalene based fuel JET B. This is because these fuels ignite at low temperatures. Unlike petrol or diesel, JET A-1 and JET B burn with controlled radiation releasing adequate heat to run planes. They neither produce smoke nor damage the hot turbine!

Find out!

When was the first air conditioner made?

19 Why are zamboni machines used?

To make ice smooth for skaters! Before 1949, while skating, the blades of skaters made grooves and bumps in the ice on rinks. Workers had to shovel away ice and spray water to make the ice smooth for skaters. This took a lot of time. So Frank Zamboni invented a zamboni machine. It has a tractor with a blade that shaves the ice smooth, a device that sweeps up the ice into a tank and an apparatus that rinses ice. This leaves a very thin layer of water that freezes within a minute making a smooth surface for skaters!

Pocket fact

Each tyre on the Zamboni machine is hand-studded. Its full set of tyres have around 400 tungsten carbide studs!

20 Why does water drip from some air conditioners?

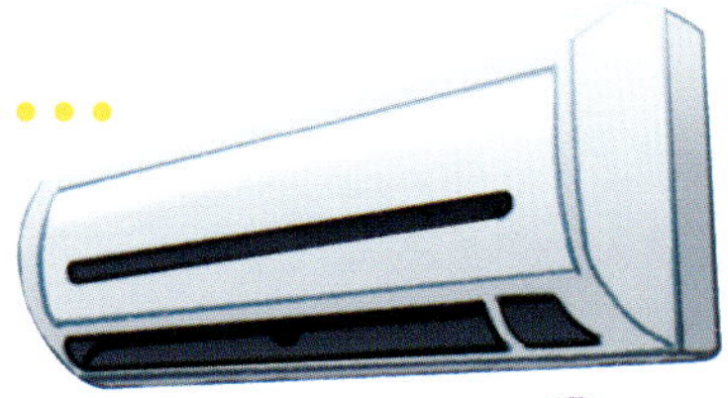

Because the air gets condensed! An air conditioner (AC) has a refrigerant that creates the cooling effect. When you switch on an AC, it sucks the air present inside the room. When air enters the AC, it is exchanged between the air and the refrigerant. The refrigerant takes away the heat from the air and cool air is blown into the room again. While air is cooled by the refrigerant, the moisture present in the air gets condensed and changes to water which drips out from your air conditioner.

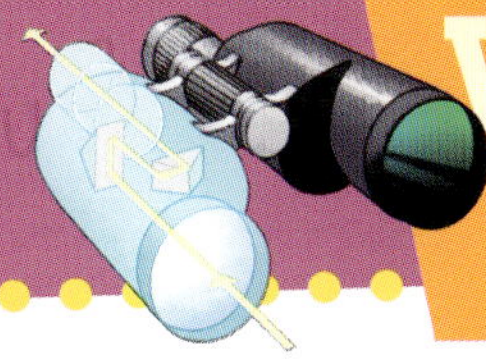

21 Why do laptops have a fan at the bottom?

To cool them! A laptop has a processor, chipset, graphics and power regulators that generate heat. The processor, chipset and graphics work at very high speeds and require a lot of power. High speed and high power requirements generate a lot of heat. The fan at the bottom keeps these systems cool, preventing your laptop from damage.

Pocket fact

The first portable computer was called GriD Compass. It was invented by British designer Bill Moggridge in 1979. But this was later improved by GRiD Systems. GRiD modified the computer into a folding screen that had a keyboard.

22 Why does a computer have ports?

To act as an interface between the computer and other devices! A computer port is a specialised outlet to which you can connect a plug or cable. Several conductors are present in the port through which cable contacts connect to the port. This provides a method to transfer signals between devices. You can connect modems, printers, mouse, and other peripheral devices to your computer with these ports.

Find out!

Who was the inventor of Kim5656890 high-voltage stabiliser?

23 Why does a CFL emit white light?

Because it emits visible light! A CFL uses an ionised gas energised by an electrical discharge to produce light. When you switch on a CFL, the electrical field accelerates free electrons. These electrons collide with gas and metal atoms and emit photons of light. These photons have visible light and ultraviolet rays. Ultraviolet rays excite the coating on the inner surface of the CFL. What you see is the visible light that is white in colour!

Pocket fact

Edmund Germer, Friedrich Meyer, and Hans Spanner were the first to make a high-pressure vapour lamp in 1927. But the first spiral CFL was invented in 1976 by Edward E. Hammer. He was an engineer with General Electric.

24 Why do some electric appliances need stabilisers?

To regulate voltage! A voltage stabiliser is a device designed to automatically maintain a constant voltage level for motor driven electric appliances like a refrigerator or air conditioner. Sometimes there is a fluctuation in the electric supply. If there is a sudden drop in voltage (usually below 220 volts), it would cause these appliances to draw more current. This may lead to overheating and thus damage the appliances.

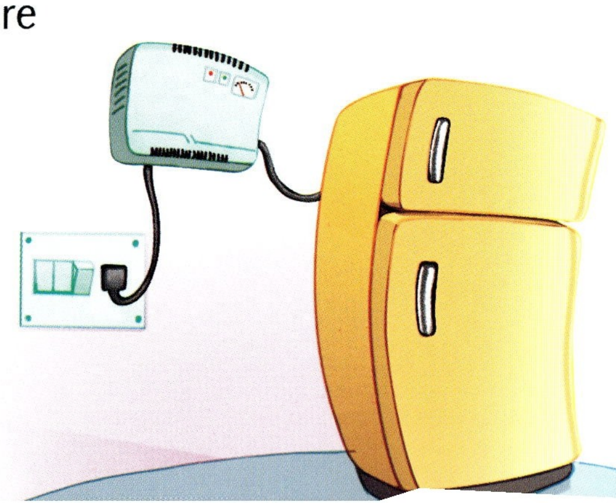

Find out!

Why are wind mills so tall?

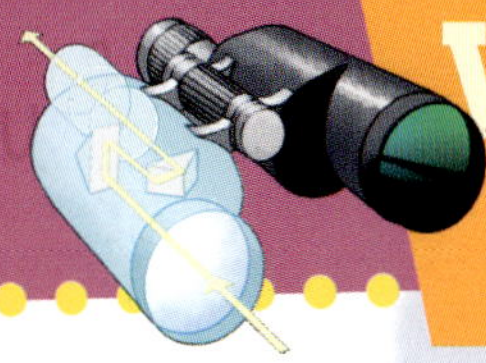

25 Why are exhaust fans fixed near the ceiling?

To drive out warm air out of the room! Warm air being light, rises up. An exhaust fan is placed near the ceiling so that it can suck the warm air out of the room, allowing fresh air to enter from elsewhere in order to replace it. The warm air that's sucked by using an exhaust fan is then pulled through a ducting system and pushed outside.

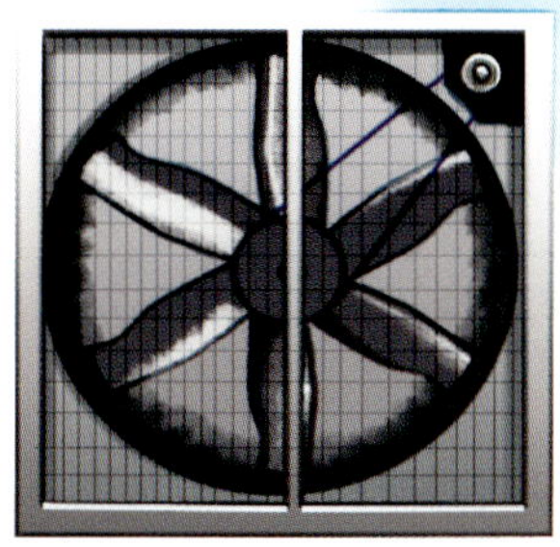

Pocket fact

Can we use fans to ventilate mines? In 1734, a Frenchman John Theophilus Desagulier invented the paddle fan to ventilate mines.

26 Why do wind turbines have gears?

To make it spin faster! A wind turbine uses wind energy to generate electricity! It has blades that rotate to capture wind. The blades of a wind turbine are attached to a shaft and turn only about 18 revolutions a minute. This is not enough to generate electricity by itself. So the turbine has a series of gears. The turbine's rotor shaft spins these gears to increase the rotation up to about 1,800 revolutions per minute. The wind turbine now has more speed and can produce a lot of electricity.

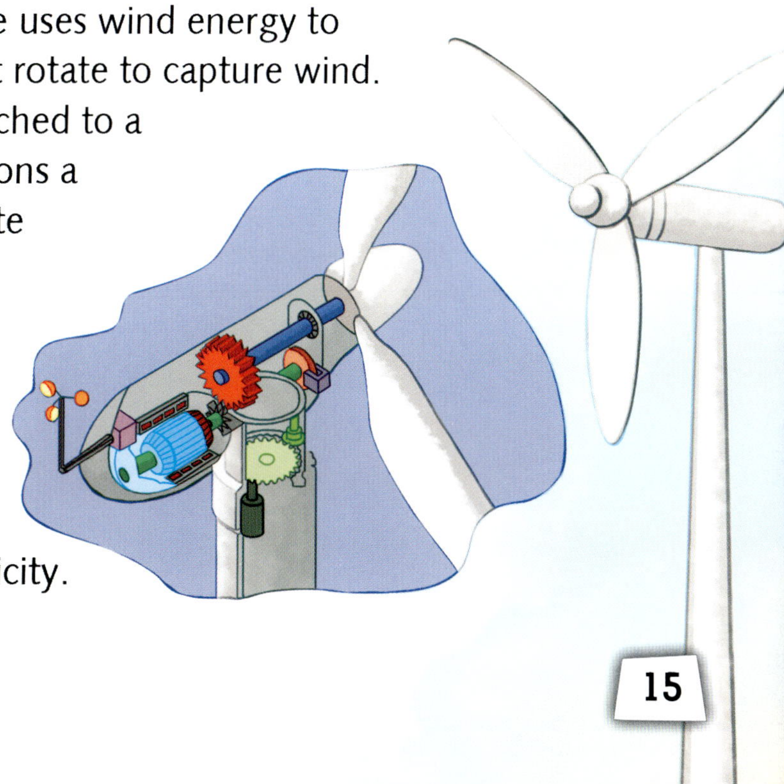

OTHER TITLES IN THIS SERIES

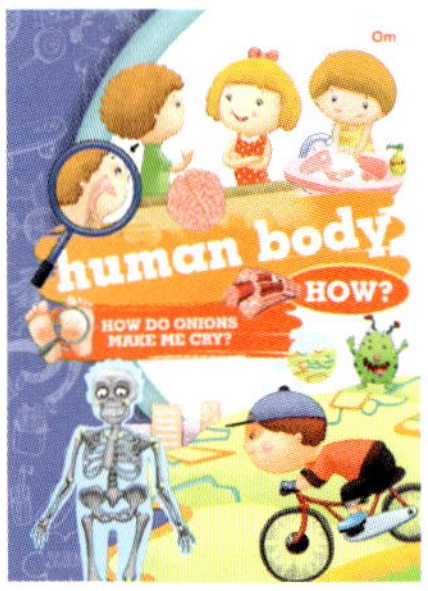

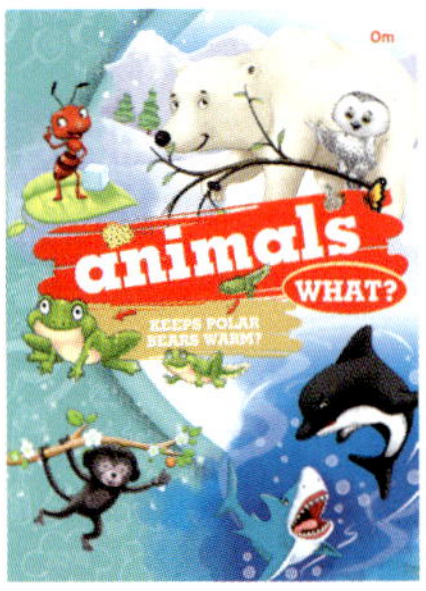

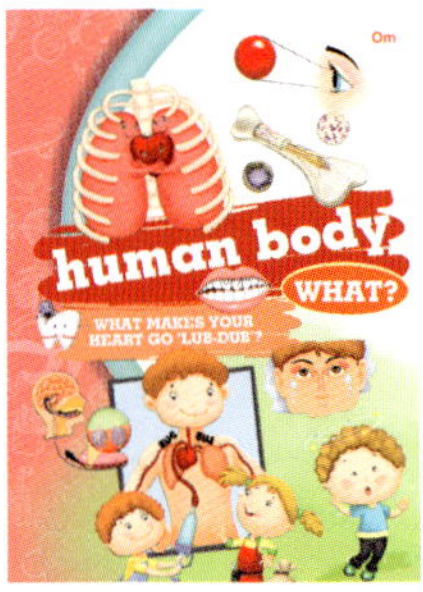

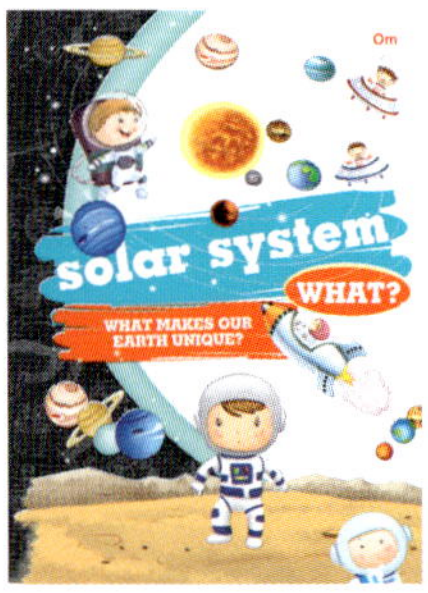

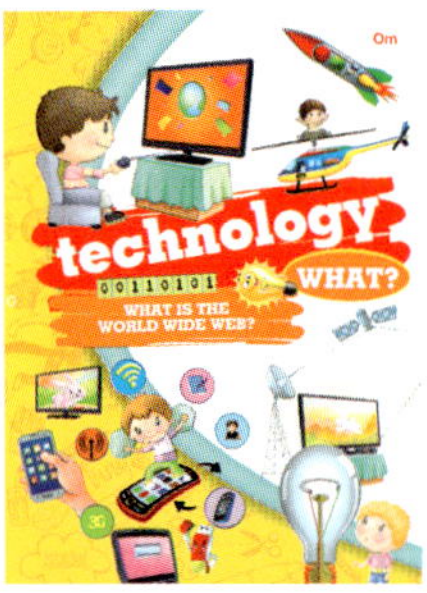

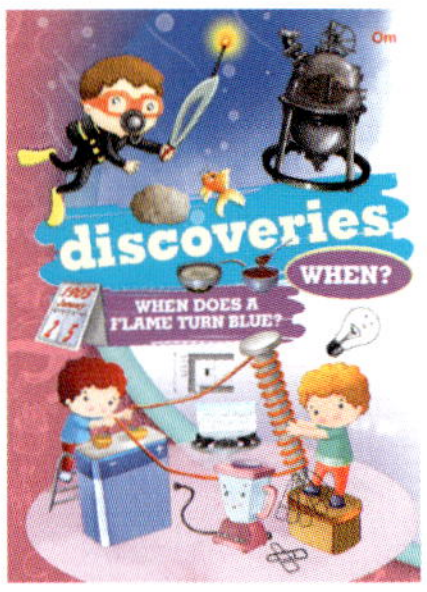

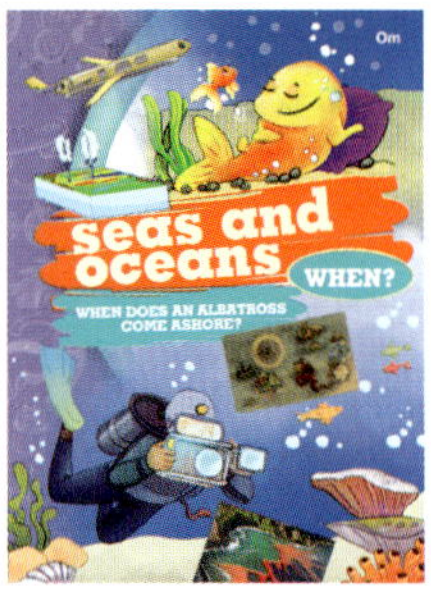

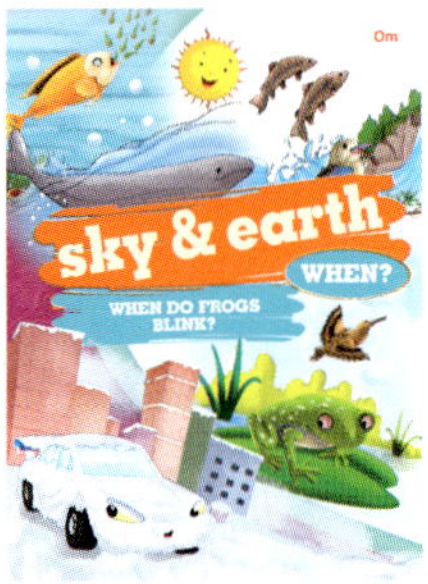

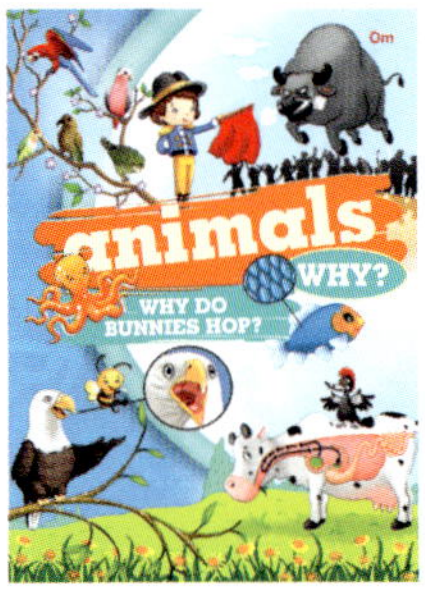

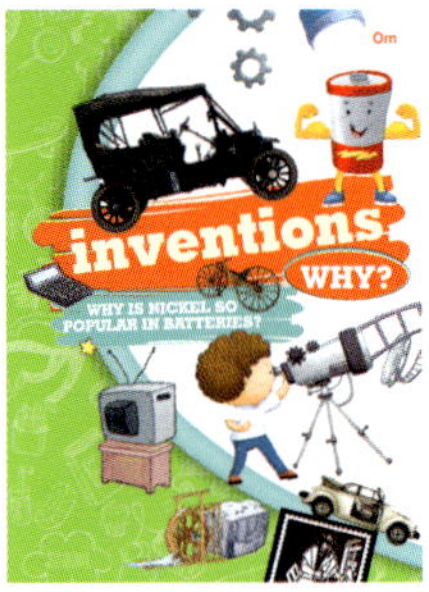

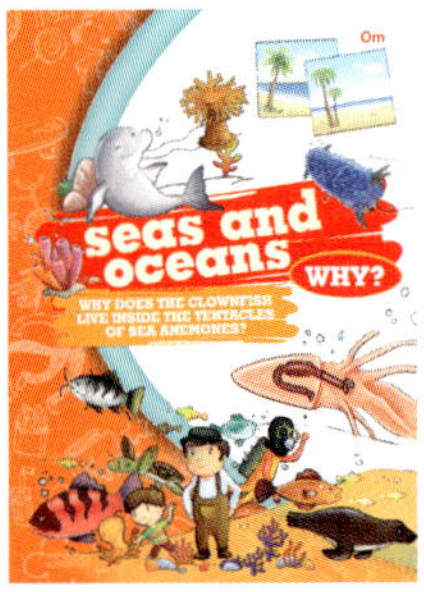

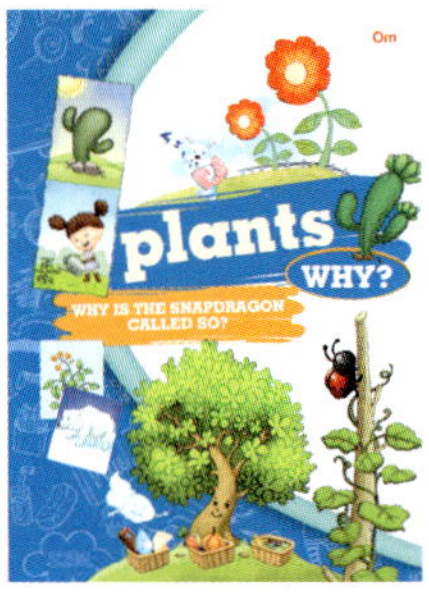